**(This Is Not A)
Mixtape for the End of the World**

(THIS IS NOT A) MIXTAPE FOR THE END OF THE WORLD

Daniel M. Shapiro

(This Is Not A) Mixtape for the End of the World

Published by bd-studios.com in New York City, 2020
Poems copyright © 2020 by Daniel M. Shapiro
Art copyright © 2020 by Stephen Tornero

Design by luke kurtis

ISBN 978-1-950231-97-3

All Rights Reserved. No part of this publication may be reproduced, stored in a retrieval system or transmitted in any form or by any means without the prior permission in writing of copyright holders and of the publisher.

This book is dedicated to these musicians who passed away too soon and who inspired many of the poems here:

Patti Donahue, Prince, George Michael, Bob Casale, Ian Curtis, Alan Myers, Michael Hutchence, David Bowie, James Honeyman-Scott, Pete Farndon, Robert Buck, Robert Palmer, Dennis Davis, Ben Orr, Ric Ocasek, Laura Branigan, and Nigel Preston.

Contents

Side A

I Found Someone	13
Talk of the Town	14
Talk Talk	15
Is There Something I Should Know?	16
A Girl in Trouble (Is a Temporary Thing)	17
Owner of a Lonely Heart	18
How Soon Is Now	20
Like the Weather	22
Mad about You	24
Running Up That Hill	26
Fire in the Twilight	27
Here She Comes	28
Rise	29
I Ran	31
Turn Back the Clock	32
I Like	34
Promises, Promises	35

Genius of Love	36
Passing Strangers	39
Too Shy	40
Why Can't I Be You?	41
Black Coffee in Bed	42
Pearly Dewdrops' Drops	43
The Killing Moon	44
Someone's Calling	45
Bedsitter	46
Touch and Go	48
Rip It Up	50
Running with the Night	52
Perfect Way	54
Take the L	56
Stand Back	58

Side B

Synchronicity II	60
Take on Me	62
Smalltown Boy	64
Heart and Soul	65
Limbo	66
Make the Weather	68
I'll Tumble 4 Ya	69
Girl U Want	71
A Little Respect	72
It's Alright (Baby's Coming Back)	73
A Different Corner	74
Kiss the Dirt (Falling Down the Mountain)	77
Eyes of a Stranger	78
Burning Down the House	80
She Sells Sanctuary	82
Just Can't Get Enough	85
In the Mood	86
I'll Be There	87
Shout to the Top	88
Far Side of Crazy	91
Gloria (a)	92
Gloria (b)	93
The Sun Goes Down (Living it Up)	94
Living in the Plastic Age	96

Saved by Zero	98
Control	100
Valerie	102
Affair of the Heart	103
Love My Way	105
Love Is a Battlefield	106
Suburbia	107
Marlene on the Wall	108
She Bop	110
Tong Poo	111
I Can't Wait	114
Hero Takes a Fall	115
Doctor! Doctor!	116
Waiting for a Star to Fall	118
What's on Your Mind (Pure Energy)	120
Don't Dream It's Over	121
Acknowledgments	122
About the Author	124
About the Artist	125

SIDE A

I Found Someone

Once upon a time there was time. People would live each day in cliché, believing breaking up mattered, cheating mattered. He danced with you while he looked at her. You kicked him out, found another who looked just like him. You cried for hours while trying to get your hair to stay big. He groped and grinded her to make you jealous. You let your new him do the same. Of course you wound up back together to tell the story we couldn't hear, we who were ducking under abandoned shelters, writhing in soot-covered beds, exorcising demons on walks through alleys. We wanted to care but had to save more than youth that wears out its welcome, as if your remake mattered more than the original.

Talk of the Town

You didn't ask to be here. The powers had told you and the band to show up on time, to remove the color from your skin. Only the drummer's outfit matters, red to draw the eye, to make beats look like blood in the binary light. The director positions you and the others on matrices, tells you not to worry about the order of operations that shift whites to blacks, blacks to whites. When the camera grabs you and won't let go, just maintain eye contact with glass until the spinning stops. You feel blades dig in, feel them turning you into the other band members, turning them into you. These are simply other matrices entering and leaving your plane. They disorient only temporarily. You're told the finished product will be magnificent; you'll block out whatever seems traumatic. You won't even remember none of this was your fault.

Talk Talk

In the beginning, one light shined down an alley, painted the outlines of moot architecture. When the band appeared—in white suits, with white instruments, in a white room—we rejoiced in the new art, farewell to the squint. We celebrated the black hat's transition to white rabbit, a lone speaker of words. Everyone else reveled in the nonverbal, turned their fatalism to sign language. They dressed alike, practiced aerobics, choreographed the lift of airships. We ignored the one casualty, the woman blinded by sunglasses, her mouth sewn shut. She appeared at the party for a millisecond, keeping complete sentences locked up, leaving her name out of the song.

Is There Something I Should Know?

You weren't allowed to remember. They brought us to the gallery, split our faces across canvases. They made us dress identically, ties tucked into shirts to keep us from choking on engines. We were placed on a giant's flayed skin, told to walk through fields of hair. You were made to look pretty, less manly, the lamb that hides its fangs. They laughed when you tried to shake your shadow. We kept looking up to see if the source of light was a way out. They said we could leave once we'd made babies from dust and clay, babies to learn from videos that looped. Pieces of our past dripped on the floor among the cigarette butts, the broken bottles. Your face froze at points of impact. They told us not to worry, that others would soon replace us. Others would shake up the art we had made, a snow globe with a hole. We would get to look back fondly, to channel the mantra of an empty room.

A Girl in Trouble (Is a Temporary Thing)

Before the nonlinear could teleport through billboards, could go from darkened swamp to safety of sunlight in an instant, all was white. The most dedicated men lay camouflaged in sand, waited to reach up, to appropriate diversity by the ankle. Others tiptoed in flannels and hats, pointed rifles, told the spectrum to freeze. They hid under splatter-painted faces, kissed women in slow motion under water out of love, out of love for the photogenic moment. No one could save the picket fences, the placeholders for boundaries. No one could rescue mouthpieces from the shooting gallery. The lucky few escaped by learning to walk on water, to extract function from blasphemy. They craved simple physics, the one-stroke linking of points, but all the colors rushed into haphazard matrices. They were forced to teleport blankly, without messages.

Owner of a Lonely Heart

Like all of us, he begins as a dot; the crowd would retain its definition without him. He knows gaslight only as a noun. When the eye zooms in to make out his identity, two men emerge to grasp his arms, to rush him to trial. He begins to replace what his eyes know, washes his face with maggots. The only faith he owns is the tickle of tarantula. He is sentenced for implanted crimes, tossed in a descending elevator, a blatant message. Unwilling to wait, to replay the force of claws on bare skin, he escapes to a rooftop. Suited men surround him, animals turned to men turned to animals, a line over a number after a decimal point. His faith looks past the suits to skyscrapers, to the don't-look-down. He knows what a leap would be for a man. He knows. Midway through the rush toward sidewalks, toward the hair-covered tops of dots, he becomes the hawk he had always believed in. Floating against traffic, he will live to consume the larvae of nightmares.

How Soon Is Now

You get to be the woman whose story is told in frames, in still images that appear to fuse. You make up your mind to put your whole being into every frame in case it ends before you're ready. First you look into the camera while you dance. This seems like a practice take, so after several seconds of watching the band play, you dance again. Now the guitarist teaches the lead singer to finger a few chords. These men have used up your time, so you vow to show them on your next turn. Now you're not black and white like you used to be; your hair is the color of those sugar cookies Mom used to make, your sweater home-for-holidays red. You forgot to dance that time.

A bunch of your frames go to the smokestacks that spew black-gray on white-gray. Then you have a symbolic breakthrough, opening three doors. More band, more factories, more you dancing. You try to speak but don't have enough time to complete a sentence before your life cuts away. You realize you have set unrealistic goals for yourself, spend the closing moments looking in the mirror, closing the door you had thought was more than one. And then the credits roll, the names of only band members etched in all caps.

Like the Weather

All the drones like her. Men try to fight them with bats or broom handles, wind up with holes in their necks. She smiles at the whir of metal, knows what ashen skin in a red dress can do to tiny green eyes. A swirl of confetti slips through her window; raindrops fall indoors. She keeps hearing the music after it stops, keeps twirling while the wind kneads her hair.

At times the machines aren't sure about her. She can get bored, turn colors to binary. When the machines read black and white, they slip into sleep mode. Even in their weakened settings, her smile never leaves her face, body never leaves home. Good attention and bad attention sleep on the same silk sheets, no need for elsewhere when the camera makes house calls. She is nonstop movement, a voice that pushes the range before it forgets to breathe. Her inevitable rush of pink on white will lift their heads, call them back to their calling.

Mad about You

I used to be in love with the West Coast. She would send me letters, vintage celluloid scraped with a snipped nail. I could watch her dance on the beach, an itch of cinema nostalgic for smog. At first, she touched me like the magic hour. I would let the West Coast smoke in bed. I didn't care when she dished my specifics over coffee with her best friend, didn't care when she let another man walk through her fields of hair. All I needed was for the West Coast to look over her shoulder, to breathe in my sunlight as we pricked our tongues on cliffs. I still don't know where she went, if she ghosted me. She could have fallen into the sea as the B movies foretold, carried the hours of rush hour with her. Now I walk as the others walk, recalling a convertible I drove only in circles, the unfinished embrace of salt and sand.

Running Up That Hill

The powers don't approve of how man and woman make excuses with light. Dancers wear skintight gray in a room without electricity. Call it contemporary so one can begin where the other begins, no need for the patriarchy of lifts. In school, emotion was a synonym for conflict, depth for abandonment. Now the powers gift them with populations of masks, meditation fit for a dollhouse. When their faces finally blossom, makeup of the day narrowing the identifiable contours, metallic eyes will scan the duplicates. They will search for misalignment, signs of care. The man and woman will be left to find slivers of mirror, to bloody fingers for seconds of vanity.

Fire in the Twilight

The powers treated him as one of them, gave him the authority to reverse. He restored coffee and toast to the man who dropped his tray, returned the bloodied biker to two wheels without a scratch. Unsure how to control it, he avoided cemeteries, steered clear of exes. He felt manipulated but couldn't turn them down. Who wouldn't relish the chance to strategize, to be on time for meetings, to win all the game shows. Months in, all the fine-tuning, the revisions of how to live had made him the most productive, most efficient. Now he built all the machines by himself, no repairs needed. At the end of each workday, he would rewind, start again, his life a loop of perfection.

Here She Comes

The question doesn't matter. The answer depends on which version of yourself you want to destroy. The one dressed in black wakes the stone soldiers, restores color to red coats and camo. The soldiers march behind and ahead of you. They don't defend or attack. The you dressed in white never leaves her car, chases you into a warehouse with nothing inside. Black-dressed you finds another car, speeds after who sped after you until one of you crashes. One of you explodes. You think you're the one wearing black, but you don't feel like the western movie archetype, the bad guy. You can't bring yourself to look at your clothes. All you see is white smoke. All you feel are gears that won't shift, the stalled engines of misplaced wars.

Rise

People once walked past people they thought *looked homeless*. Then the powers made men in business suits homeless. With time recalibrated, the women washed laundry by hand, put it out to dry near the men in suits. The powers called this a return to old-fashioned values. The only band left had accordion, tuba, upright bass, fiddle, the last sign of punk rock, the first sign of punk rock, dirty- and sad-faced, fired by its leader when his hair turned orange. This leader had been homeless when he poked holes in shirts and eyebrows, when it was OK to say looked homeless. Now he wears a suit, lives in a castle, dreams of his mother putting out laundry when the wind would swirl, when the wind would lift a finger from his fist. He walks by the homeless, reaches into his pockets, makes sure the cash stays covered.

I Ran

His days form a circumference, radius drawn from eye contact. He speaks only of running, of escaping the beams. Eventually, the light from each outside eye becomes a woman. He had always wanted two, wanted to show them what he could do with one finger on a key. His nerves make him slip into the dark space where mirrors don't see. Ultimately, he reappears, unable to isolate himself from his own reflections. The women half-smile, wishing they'd put on makeup for someone other than themselves, for someone who would dare to leave the circle. Only when they return to the stars does he try to run to them, but the formula won't allow. Leaving the center would trip the shriek of sirens. The ratio must remain the same, proportions intact. No one stays long enough to touch.

Turn Back the Clock

In prison, his job is to check machines, to make sure nostalgia has been removed. What he had done couldn't happen again: no more sitting in the last pickup, imagining to be one of the boys walking by. Secrets lived in someone else's tree house. To think you peaked in youth is to languish in a cell. Because of him, no one can get away with pretending, with remembering how they loved abusive fathers, pranks at their expense.

Some of the programmers couldn't resist, setting up machines to miss restaurants that had burned down, athletics played for money. Uniquely capable of turning memories to happy lies, he can match them electrode for electrode, can identify the tiniest feelings with no purpose. He learned to curve his mind, to listen for commands such as *go to the store*, to make sure they don't really mean *describe that store I used to go to when I was 6*. Vehicles are to turn right *in 500 feet*, not *where people leaned in chairs to watch motion pictures*. He is new at it but almost where they want him, almost able to forget what it feels like to wear clothes that fit.

I Like

The powers wanted to see how big a disease had to be to spark a renaissance. They electrified lutes, cross-pollinated harpsichords and Moogs. The masses squeezed into the venue, all-access passes promising signed merchandise. The masses were handed syringes labeled *authentic warhead*. To get to the stage, they would need to evade men in riot gear, men too confident to breathe; jump barriers that looked like steel but were blood-whiffing sharks crisscrossed into bars; scale barbed wire that needed no disguise. The band would bring out the frenzy, any misstep turning their cables to scourges. Each time a crowd succumbed, another was brought in, first set into second set, chaperons and hennins covering all the scattered scars of artists.

Promises, Promises

They will put you in prison for losing at solitaire, for voicing pool-boy fantasies—dealing chlorine to a woman with matching red suit and towel. Over time, the water will slowly turn to a canvas of sky blue, clouds moving too quickly, like blood that lets go. The woman you made up will float face down in the center. No one will come to your defense. No one will point out the skimmer was always a paintbrush, never a knife. The powers maintain you did the unspeakable: You stole the grind from a dance floor, mistook the crass for sublime. When you're sentenced to the thoughts they give, you'll forget what it means to appeal, remembering only what had been real: the stillness of the diving board, stripes on a life ring untouched.

Genius of Love

This doesn't happen when you wake up. You don't wake up when you never sleep. This that happens is what used to be in the notebooks, the cartoons that got you through the boring classes. Your skyscrapers dance in a flipbook, dance the same way they did when they made you laugh. When it's all a cartoon, you just watch open-mouthed. You and your friends stand behind bars you forget to erase. You stand behind the lines that hide mouths and noses, which you can't draw as well as necks and legs. You are better off without a mouth or nose. These drawings of dogs, of basketball players, of your city dancing, they flip by too quickly. You sit in the apartment with just enough light to see the pages, with just enough light to check vital signs. The flipping of the book is the only motion. Were you to dare to look outside, you would see what's flatter than a trail of graphite, dustier than dropped pastels. Now you feel your moot mouth tighten. You lick a hole in the candy you drew. You remember the real candy tasted like blank paper.

Passing Strangers

Underground, he and she mime, silent film stars without an audience. Colors exist only where they don't want to go. Soon the couple withdraw their jagged moves inspired by the robots they had seen when there was TV. Now they dwell on what's easiest: their shadows from the one light that's on, the first dance they ever learned. Mid-waltz, their salvaged stream of white is interrupted by men who rattle and bounce. He and she don't have time to determine what helps, what hurts, so they run. They stay hand in hand and run. When they reach the surface, succumb to natural light, blood brings them the pinks and reds they had missed. A blast in their footprints adds orange. Black and white will return in the shape of smoke, the lost cigarettes of prehistoric studios.

Too Shy

These were baby's first sounds. No one likes when they grow, when they place choruses where verses should go. Lost are the wispy hair, scent of life before irony. People who see braids dangle from mullets will side with machines. To flaunt exposed roots is to hold guitars too high, to turn *catchy* into *curse*. What would you sell to have just one hit, to be a punch line. What would it take to make *Daddy* baby's first word, to christen a deadbeat as the new role model.

Why Can't I Be You?

When you recorded the song, they told you to turn keyboards into horns. Modern soundscapes meet swing time swagger. You had heard about dressing cute, bears and bumblebees, men as women. A band mate would wear a red lip costume, 6 feet vertically. You weren't comfortable with the opening and closing, the cuteness descending. Then they told you to darken your face, to pantomime the fingerings of the horn you'd made from keyboards. This was their vision: A famous jazz man returns from the dead to repave fractured scat vocals with electronics. You had been singled out, the second coming of the first great soloist. At the screening, you marveled at your image, at how different this was from the real you, at how much you appeared to enjoy the slathering on of a culture.

Black Coffee in Bed

The sneaks and snitches made this happen. They sold the secrets of time door to door, ruled the apartment complex with a musician in every other window. If they didn't like a man, they would slip him a mickey, watch him go from grope to marriage to baby to affair to breakup in a day. Fueled by the shortening of seconds, bands loudly turned planets to shrunken heads. They drew the attention of the powers, who boarded up the complex, tried to torture out truths but couldn't lengthen the pain. They had no way to infiltrate memories. All they could do was lock up the hooligans, hire drum machines off the street, pay top dollar for the most beats per minute. The new music would play at factories, where workers would tighten clamp tighten clamp tighten clamp to the relentless thumping of innovation.

Pearly Dewdrops' Drops

You're told your voice can be the only voice, a single layer of skin regrown each hour. At first your band records in a church, but the ghosts callus the mix with whispered prayers. Dice clutter the game board of stained-glass panes. Only one place would remove the melee from echoes, highballs that never stay empty long enough. The powers move the sessions to the sky, where blue can be the only color, air thin enough to tame each overdub. Your voice will never go raw again, preserved on subzero reel-to-reels as each photon of the sun forms a backing track. With wings tucked in, you would never leave.

The Killing Moon

The man sat alone with more dread than water to drink. He chose to run out the clock rather than help the plan, rather than follow the instructions for how to build a boat from fear: *1.) Fashion the threat of war into booms and masts. 2.) Cover the threats in opaque sheets that shimmer as they hide. 3.) Exclude the deck; plan to levitate passengers over water, to make them look down. 4.) Swing an overhead lamp from a wire; tell them it's the moon chastising the sea. 5.) Hire a captain who won't say a word, who will never show his face. 6.) Let your boat be propelled by the promise of rescue, of well-earned closure.* He took pride in remaining on land, sharks surrounding him only when he closed his eyes. He thrived on the failure of sleep.

Someone's Calling

You can't make out the whole headline, just the word *break*. Red lights rotate and scream to fill in the blanks. All you're trying to do is get to the gig, where the women tease their hair. You're afraid of what will happen when you bring them home, when the whiteness reveals the parts of your face that aren't close to perfect. You will want to wrap yourself in bandages, depart to the sarcophagus you've stocked with wine coolers and headphones. This fate would be superior to the running, the puddle of sprint like criminals who tunnel back to prison. No one should have to worry this much, so you stay out late by yourself. No one should have to make out what can't be put together.

Bedsitter

They say the famous river formed when somebody left the faucet on, partied too much, forgot where home was. Back then, all people did was wait in their pajamas until nighttime came. They formed synth pop duos to afford eyeliner, placed their shirtsleeves on layaway. Everyone saw them on the subway but couldn't recognize them; they were followed only from behind, speed-walking ahead from loneliness to Top of the Pops. They pretended not to know where love went, worshiped boys who thought they were vampires but didn't need stakes through hearts to die. The powers accused them of cultural appropriation without adequate cover, marked them for death, but their curated cries of soul singers drowned in four feet of tap water, while the river smirked at the droplets' applause.

Touch and Go

A band of men is given carte blanche to make its own propaganda. The band of men looks nervous. Too much freedom can make people nervous. The powers try to relax the band: *You'll feel better if you picture everyone in their underwear. His or her underwear.* The band of men pictures its members on a record label, pictures how the spin is like a carousel. The music changes, but the label of men keeps going to the same 360 degrees' worth of places and returning to the beginning. The men don't want to be the label. They remember their carte blanche, make a video of themselves on a carousel. Women ride the carousel, women in only their underwear. Now the men are nervous again, watching the women go up and down on horses. After a few turns, the powers have amassed enough film and begin to apply adhesive to the men's backs. The powers wait until the last second to hand the women their clothes as the rotation slows to stillness, all the horses fixed midair.

Rip It Up

Our drummer clues us in to the classified: *Band wanted to perform on space station for study of zero-gravity fingerings and poses.* The powers make clones of us to entertain Earth. We will be able to watch ourselves via satellite, conspicuous in matching beach shirts and hats while the population bundles up. Amps and tom-toms cling to the floor our feet never touch. After floating in a box for days, we stop feeling the electrodes. We sleep with guitars grafted on belt buckles, wake when our cheeks brush the ceiling. Now we see ourselves dressed as frogmen on city streets. We wonder when the powers will show us holding hands with partners, dropping our kids off at school. One hundred million miles from our planet, the voice in the earpiece tells us to go to the foil-walled compartment. We will test the effects of heat on charisma. As we become transparent in an experiment of light, our Earth selves practice their next pratfalls.

Running with the Night

The powers chose him to teach the replacements to walk. They had seen his work on a seized videocassette: In the near darkness of indeterminate past, he primps in a mirror, carefully tilts a fedora, leaves his room. Then, in a series of flourishes, he shuts his door, knocks on the one across the hall, extends his arm high, bends it to form a triangle with elbow-hand-armpit vertices, offers it to the woman leaving her room. Before the tape goes blank amid the blasphemy of guitar solo, this man—this human—has trained an army of dancers to overthrow human marriage.

After they have been altered by the powers, human men will be fitted with fedoras to hide the handiwork. They will collect abandoned parts, bring them to the factories where they work until the ephemera breaks down. The replacements, without the burden of music to feel rhythm, will perform the most precise tasks in unison: liquid crystal surgeries, power-supply upgrades, corrosion checks. Occasionally one of them will glitch, reaching chrome fingers to where its throat would be. It will pull at a phantom necktie, one part masculine style, one part seizing of breath.

Perfect Way

Of course everyone leaves. The best we can get is to remember the ones made fun of, to decipher words left to die, plastic shovels under sand. What if no one had noticed when the phoenix rose, no one had recognized the meaning of the mural in the church that showed men pointing at each other? The disembodied mistook them for break dancers transferring energy.

We know God gave Adam syncopation, warned him to beware the thieves of rhythm. We took drum kits for granted until they became extinct. Programmed beats had begun their rise to power long before synth-pop syndicates turned in their souls, long before garages had ceased to echo. It took only a day for the metal tendrils to run through all the instruments, through all the musicians.

Shrewd cult figures crammed into time capsules without a shred of sweat, DNA firewalled with only buttons to think-push, buttons to mimic the present tense. Humanity would be left to slither in sound-proof armor, to stretch plastic across black market cylinders. All would be committed to mp3 and promptly incinerated, metronome of work overlapping the real art, ashes to flight.

Take the L

They told her she could tell her life story as a comic book. They vowed not to interfere. Page One, Frame One: Boyfriend kisses her when she doesn't want to be kissed. Screen-printed on boyfriend's shirt is a target. Page One, Frame Four: Boyfriend reacts to rejection, throws beer bottle through TV screen. Page Two, Frame Three: She invites him to the bar, goes to the bar, a neutral place to break up. Page Two, Frame Four: He hugs her too tightly.

In a few pages, they have taken over. We see her crying, swimming in a dark sea. Unable to bear living without him, she slips under the water. Even they can't end it this way, so they offer a parallel reality, drop her off on a lonely road with only one suitcase. They lose interest in the final third, rely too much on incongruent frames: breaking glass, kabuki makeup, mystery man. They flash a life before your eyes, a life unfinished. They let her live so she may mourn all her lives let go by men.

Stand Back

We become victims by being forced to play victims. The powers tell you you're nothing without a partner, be it God or a model with a waxed chest. They think they can wrap me in low-cut lace, make me walk the treadmill in heels to electrify their suites. More agreeable duplicates wait in the greenroom, prepared to lip-sync my words. From the front row, the powers watch the agony of my eyes, label me hysterical, shrill, entranced. As students of dance contests, of sweat shops, they envision my punishment. The powers have read up on how long it takes for fires to engulf a body of my shape and size. They have not found my diaries the doves lifted to the skies. No one can exorcise my spells, the notes I have yet to sing. I will continue to spin like a sphere beyond the telescope's reach. Only the words they'll never see can stop that rotation, that swagger I cloak in the cutwork of twitches.

SIDE B

Synchronicity II

They put us here as punishment for smuggling images from homicidal books. We started out naked, stretched on abandoned girders, left to reel in torn textiles of every color. The wind stopped twice a day for system maintenance. They stretched tubes from the oceans to our throats, fed us climate change to aid in the digestion of hammerheads. Some days our hair spiked white, barbed wire to trap us on islands. They built our prison bars with the only Stratocasters in tune, topped them with streamers rendered from seized cassettes. Our guitarist pulled a steel rod from the heap, made frets from discarded phalanges.

Their mistake was to leave us the parts that fit the formula: *cyclone + blades + ghosts = electricity*. Surveillance showed only my front-man sneer, too theatrical to flash the hand of anarchy. The first chord we could amplify tripped the escape hatch, the path to many miles away. We would leave sleep to the professionals.

Take on Me

When your whole life is a pre-existing condition, it's hard to find a taker. He had been living frame by frame, charcoal on paper. She just wanted to finish her coffee, remain three-dimensional. Synthesizers can play in both worlds, but police are only black and white. When his ghastly pale hand rose from the page, of course she took it. When you've been trained to dress in beige, you'll take it. She must've known the pursuit of love was a crime, running at the first sight of authority. But this would be no flat Romeo, even after she had crumpled him, left him for dead. He would find a way to pressurize, craft his own lungs, acclimate to melanin. She knew every equation was perfect; only the solutions were a mess. After the whens had expired, they met again in color, her turn to reach out, introduce both of them to dangers, wayward pastels.

Smalltown Boy

This young man didn't need the powers. He had his own father. This young man was guilty of riding a train and looking straight through the window, mistaking the speeding landscape for progress. He stopped at a pool, watched another man dive in, watched this man's legs tip too far forward, forgave the imperfection. This young man saw the other man return his lock-eyed lust. He couldn't have expected the mob led by that man, the mob that kicked the lack of fear into a fetal ball. This young man got back on the train, saw the trees, the smoke, the clouds as one simple picture, simple as the crumpled bill his father gave him to move out, no longer welcome. He got back on the train, heard the sound of a voice warning him of closing doors. He knew keeping his gashed face in full view would eventually make them open.

Heart and Soul

Dance had been legalized but only if performed in shadows. Born in a room's dark corner, she had been the first triple-helix to survive. They would have dispensed with her had she not tripped their sonogram eyes to code red. The halo that had burned them proved their polymers could bond with blood. Because enough of them was inside her, they had to let her live in exile. She would whisper through life as pregnant girls did in ancient times—keep the smoking-gun glow under loose clothing. She learned to embrace DNA, to care less about the lingering taste of what used to be called synthetic. Whatever tried to bully her would walk away slowly, arms in need of a solder. She had shouted a flow chart to mark the steps of how to beg, Prometheus with all the inviting organs intact.

Limbo

The weakest of men lowers a lamp to the ground, molds his shadow three stories tall. He puts a leash on a numbed beast, walks it down Main Street in broad daylight. To set traps for the illegally blind, he dresses women in handprints, reads body temperatures for spikes. *Life is more beautiful as a black-and-white photo*, he thinks as he retrofits the rods and cones of guests. Sure he remembers hunger, the stench of ponies on his father, who walked home from the farm. He wants you to know he always asks, always asks the women to dance because he can't. *You must fill the space of what you can't do.* He covers his tracks with too many session players. *Only you know if you love someone, if you've watched love stand naked with cash on the floor.* He knows money buys the illusion of more money. *When you remove chance, you create perfection, the bliss inside the vacuum.* He knows money is the opposite of voodoo, knows that when the powers come for him, they'll find a tuxedo gored by a dozen high heels.

Make the Weather

All the fears had been outsourced, shaped into spheres in space. The powers awaited their return, nuggets of anxiety speeding like the speech of stars. We hid behind pinholed boxes to track the emotional eclipse. For a few minutes the whole world vented, raged at curlers held in hair too long, vandalism to undertake in broad daylight. We escaped the outside to plug in: cords from instruments to amps, through walls to the machine that ushered in the blue-black serenity. Our machine-made problems go the way of ice caps. We lulled with a monotone of rust, danced the twist while the powers looked us up and down, the twist of heels into cloven hooves. The sting of our bass lines crawled up their vertebrae, numbed their templates from the neck down. Umbrellas as tight as our rhythm section deflected the contrived imprint of their legacy.

I'll Tumble 4 Ya

They invite you to a variety show. You're overcome with admiration as you watch everyone warm up: fire eaters' unlit run-throughs, jugglers' tosses of turned-off chainsaws. *Stay backstage*, they say. As a White Swan *pas de deux* ends, they say, *Now it's your turn*, push you onto the stage. You start to walk off and they say, *Don't make us show you what happens to the losers*. You're about to ask what you're supposed to do when the piano player starts to play boogie-woogie and nods at your feet. You don't know how you were outfitted with tap shoes, don't know how the Bandy twists and barrel rolls come so easily. The audience nearly drowns out your sound but restrains itself enough to hear the rhythms you had held inside for your whole life. As your feet continue to move, you know you must be the winner. You try not to think about what will happen to the sword swallowers and unicyclists, but you love to win.

Girl U Want

By day they swapped lyrics while inspecting carcasses, layers beneath treads and sidewalls. The steady buildup of rolling machines funded their nights under energy domes, nights dipped in deep violet stage presence. Rubber and steel stretched from KV-4000 to holes in the hats of break dancers. The cries of young women lulled hexane and toluene into trances, stifled the grind of synthetics on foreheads. The women held up signs to spark backstage after-parties, signs that hinted at special talents: elliptical engineering, force field aligning, prosthetic sorting. Who wouldn't brave the dangers of vulcanizing for opportunities, opportunities for art, scorched polymers that shrink like hem lines.

A Little Respect

When a man lives in a kaleidoscope, he's not allowed to sit still. He envies the black-and-white life, what others take literally. Those who dwell outside grow tired of his mockery, his spoken words with subtitles in the same language. He says *sweeter* while pouring sugar in a teacup, *respect* while holding a sign that says *respect*. His friend visits, considered too pretty to be a threat. He dons costumes to mingle with diversions, the warriors, the skeletons. The powers had forgotten prison breaks are best executed in twos. They had closed their eyes while the friends dismantled words, removing a single letter from each. Gibberish melded into hammers, broken consonants into frequencies that sounded like keyboards. The beautiful men smashed through eons-rendered chromatics, basked in the freedom of white light.

It's Alright (Baby's Coming Back)

Of course we should've experimented beyond the vocoder. You played the oceans through my headphones while I slept, told me to lie still as my body rose from my body. When my new layer awoke, I saw you only as a shadow. Our dimensions newly reduced, we hugged awkwardly but meant well. The horn arrangements gave me a pulse, helped me picture where my heart was supposed to be. I never liked ribs, never trusted cages. You thought I looked too pale so you drew me a hospital, rushed me there in an oversized car of one unbroken line. You didn't have to fold me. Now I'm the way everyone expects me to be except when my sight goes flat, when colors go primary. Shapes can lose their ambiguous edges. Eventually my eyes reclaim their curves, lungs their chance to hold notes, to hold sighs. Of course it was worth all the side effects.

A Different Corner

This is where they put you when you think you're alone. They leave you with white: uneven cushions for sleeping, stairs that lead to a lost landing. You hear cellos meant to soothe, long notes that stretch over keys, the only keys. A white telephone would let you complain to friends about loneliness, but the rotary dial won't turn. You get to wear a white sweater, cutwork embroidered, holes carved into fancy shapes. White pants are fine during any season. Best of all is a window with light that comes through, a window without the hassle of a view. Light comes through until nighttime laughs at you, shaping pieces of stars into words: *So you thought you were lonely before.* They will let you pass the time by feeling your stubble grow. Of course they can't give you a razor. When you lean against the white pillar, strike a pose that indicates authentic despair, they move you to a new room. This one is decorated in whatever colors bring out forgotten pictures, exposures of self-awareness.

Kiss the Dirt (Falling Down the Mountain)

When the camera flies over, it will flag us under *loss*. We begin apart, soloists who seem to sing to keep our minds off dying in white sands. As the sky darkens, we move closer together without the need for microphones, amplifiers. Time, the only metronome that matters, moves at the same rate for all of us. Machines and their instructions flash by—headlights, road signs, engines. They've come to rescue us, to return us to what we're expected to be. We ignore them, build a bonfire to light our fingerings, the beating of drums. By the time the hot sun has returned, we're still playing, accompanied by the smoke of yesterday's angels. This time, the camera rushes off to report us as outlaws or undead, as if such a distinction mattered. Music is all the water we need, the mountain in which to blend, from which to rise with shoulders high.

Eyes of a Stranger

He slept in the projection booth, awoke when the take-up reel spooled the ending in a rhythmic scold. The powers forbade the display of their image. He'd locked himself in to find evidence. Filmmakers would sneak single frames into blockbusters, one-sixteenth of a second of car chase stowaway. They knew the risk of identifying the real killer, knew the portal would open and close at the same time. All he had to do was stay up, squint through a magnifying glass, check each one by hand. The static images chilled him, swept him to the side like a one-sheet. Once he got them moving, the long takes of old did him in. Raised by the quick cut, he understood the shot reverse shot of intimacy, life of a cameo. Unconditional giving mesmerized him, how one spool passes itself to another until it's gone. Through the window, he read a blank screen's lips. Enemies would remain without faces as he dwelled on the only light in the room, reached out to it, held on long after the burn had closed its eyes.

Burning Down the House

They lied to you about the destruction, about the blink of day to night. We played to an audience of static, not smoke. The men in white suits never came for us. We wore the white, the permanent surrender, took shelter in the peacock of stained-glass window. We lacked the oxygen to catch fire, choked through calisthenics while someone else's match exhaled. Our bodies snapped into position, the last semblance of upright.

We hope you never find out what it's like to have your face placed on another face, to feel another voice when you sing. A fire's shadow doesn't burn. The reflection of a band plays only one dimension per ear. These are the words of a man whose head can't find its body. There's no *we* anymore, band scattered like a rifled pigeon. What's left of me speeds along the highway swallowing white stripes, blurring the spaces where they force you to stay.

She Sells Sanctuary

After the seas dried out, the last pirate who ever lived rolled a barrel of saltwater he had seized, stopped only to spray his body so he wouldn't die. *A pirate who steals the sea puts himself out of business.* He collected smoothed coral, skull hats, microphone stands. *A pirate who gives away the earth isn't worth his weight.* He could eat rotting fish because true scavengers side-eye bacteria. *A pirate cleans up only for the open casket.* He danced by kicking his good leg into the sand, sang through a hole no longer used for breathing. *A pirate sees the beauty of the world through a patched eye.* He forgot which letter marked the spot, remembered when waves had turned to snowsqualls overnight. *A pirate makes songs out of hollow bodies.* His big score was a single pearl in 41 million square miles of empty shells. *A pirate sees a flash of gold before he drowns.* When his barrel ran out, the pearl rested in his open hand, a blindfold nailed to the plank.

Just Can't Get Enough

We all know someone who's the umbrella in the alcoholic's drink. The band we like smiles at 128 bpm while its minds creep, while directors shoot/reverse-shoot keyboards that change the subject. Women might seem better at it, caking on more makeup than men, making watchers whisper the wrong questions. *How can she even smile?* elbows past *How will they survive?* Fun that doesn't look like self-destruction dances in tall boots until it falls. Some of the best contracts are signed at bars, in bathrooms. If it weren't dressed in black and white, it wouldn't be a cliché, the head that bobs like a metronome before nodding out.

In the Mood

We are the distractors, the ones who make you feel even less than entitled. We break down what's in your nature—the trees, the ocean—strip light into geometric shapes. You fail to recognize you're seeing mere triangles, a dance of badges the sun doesn't need anymore. We pretty the water droplets, drizzle them down metal cobwebs until you transfix, ignore the flood. Appealing to the guilt, we provide you with a woman to rescue from an empty castle, a troupe of dancers whose skin looks nothing like yours, whose art exists only for you to enjoy. It's your duty to save, to believe conscience is responsibility, fantasy a verb. You insert yourself into the landscape, take credit for lost cultures. Long after you've discovered fear, you will stumble upon a mirror, watch your face descend into a thousand circles of true color.

I'll Be There

Once I walked inside your eye. You kept your girlfriend in there, the one you always talked about. She wears a red dress, lives in a bed underwater, celebrates her birthday with a panpipe–bass drum serenade. Of course she can breathe. You know how she got there but don't like to talk about it. It must have been a spell because she can't leave like I can. They couldn't charge you with kidnapping. They called her on the water phone; she said she was fine. You sit around with candles and emote, but she's fine. You can see only what's outside your eye, so I take pictures while I'm in. Don't look at them until I'm gone. No one likes a man who puts out candles with tears. No one likes a man who lights too many candles, who keeps time by tapping his foot, a man as simple as a zoom lens that pulls too quickly, an undertow.

Shout to the Top

The powers will tell us when to talk about race. Three white men and a black woman perform in a studio. Two of the men, piano player and drummer, play hard, too hard, as if they'll be abused if they put their arms down. The other white man dances, chews gum as he sings. The black woman leans on the piano until the chorus, when she walks over to the singer and backs him up. This group performs rhythm and blues made slick with strings, rhythm guitar, funky bass all outside our view. Many couldn't guess the right colors. When the song ends, white people in centuries-old clothes pose in front of a mural on the studio wall, a mural that shows a factory, dirtied workers in lighted helmets, police to keep out and in. Still the powers haven't given us a heads up. We don't know what to talk about: white people trying to make black music, a black woman staying in the background, scabs working jobs as if they truly belong. We fidget over chord progressions, irregular harmonies. We wait.

Far Side of Crazy

When the West needed rediscovery, the powers sent a clown with a camera to compile the spotless carnage. This was before viral. Reptiles ate the strings off guitars. Townspeople wandered with eyes covered to block the awkward flips from color to black & white to color. The new colonists let their hair explode, posed with mannequins for selfies. This was before selfies. Reinvention meant erasure, but not of natives. This was after immigrants started pretending to be natives. The five men who appeared to be human formed a band that could stand alone in the desert, look good in grayscale. They had not thought past the moment, past the four minutes it would take to embed the psyches of whoever was left, whoever would dare to put on the greasepaint.

Gloria (a)

What they told her: Stay in the circle. If you venture into rectangles, we'll give the song back to the foreigners; it won't match your tongue. Be cute, not sexy. Smile, but only a little. Don't maintain eye contact with the camera. You want them to like, not lust. Watch it with your hips. Leave the star-making to us. What they didn't tell her: The disco balls have been calibrated. They sync with one another, sync with glass sequins on her blouse. Long ago the masses outgrew Morse code. Every flash of light is a byte they take in, each bit stripped of silver, processed by the proper compartment. She is the instrument, the pretty assistant who draws eyes from the magician's sleeve. They will turn off their TVs, believe they've learned nothing more than a catchy tune. Descending all the matching porches, they will form a band block, march to the store, purchase the single, await further twinkles of instructions.

Gloria (b)

The band plays in the rear-view mirror. You hear music only when you're leaving. A sign says the music is more than it appears to be. The lead singer stands alone, forgets to get out of the way when crews build highways over his face. All the headlights freeze into one long shape, the fluorescent body of an eel. We're expected to pinpoint the symbol. When waterfalls cover the sky, the face returns. The singer trudges through reeds, through snow-covered wind. This is the key to survival: lending your profile to whatever landscape imposes itself on you. If you pose enough, you become the monument.

The Sun Goes Down (Living it Up)

Our bass guitar stands body up, its headstock embedded in desert clay. This is not the sword that can't be removed. Its only companion is a door with windows, a door that keeps nothing in or out. The sun is down to its last wax.

This is our new video, which runs on whatever we can burn. We throw old-time film on the bonfire, listen to frames of happy-looking people pop. These happy people used to tap dance in black and white at the wrong speed.

We don't know how we got here, how we got to the middle of the desert, why we must play our instruments on the edge of a canyon. We don't know what's plugged in or what we pantomime. We know we are feeling it.

Our funk, our words, they sound like the crack of taps on marble, the percussion of smiles. When our music turns to ash, we replant the bass in the ground, walk to the door, look through the windows for the other side. We hear strings tightening, the reaching of roots. We know:
We will disappear.

Living in the Plastic Age

They paint some white women black, turn them into tables, paint other white women brown for telephones. They say they don't see color. Synthesizers must be played with rubber gloves. They dress you in a hooded robe, show you what you think is a miniature of your city. Even the sculptures are fitted for sunglasses. The bases the space aliens attack in video games look like your city, your miniaturized city. What you think is the throb of bass of drums is the sound of your pixelated city falling square by square. They tell you it's OK; your eyeglasses are just too thick. A man will give you a ride home on a Prophet-5, show you the lights of your darkened city. You're sure these must be correct, these lights that compete with what can only be sleep.

Saved by Zero

His father always bursts in, sticks a finger too close, scolds him for wasting time on *doodles*. Continuing makes him a true artist. A half-nude model waits for him to start—a woman he likes who likes him—while he sketches a man with tightened muscles. Continuing makes him a true artist. His friends attend the show, scowl at the pieces he has made, the pieces tagged with dollar signs. Continuing makes him a true artist. Shackled hands burst through the canvas, aim for his throat.

Continuing makes him a true artist. He returns to the muscular man, stabs canvas with a hunting knife to extricate himself. Continuing makes him a true artist. He adds colors, turns himself a red mix of sunburn and exhaustion, makes a beach of rainbows to climb. He must purge saltwater from lungs, cool the sand with his feet, grow fruit trees from sweat, fashion a hut from all the fingers thrust in his face. He will make civilization rise from a studio of doubt. Continuing makes him true art.

Control

She tells Mom and Dad she wants out, wants to ride a trapeze into fire. This is what is called independence. When she leaves her girlhood home, men in dusters and hats, men in dusters, hats, and sunglasses arrive. They all talk the same like they're friends. Like the sort of human men who aren't around anymore, they joke with her about her body, take her somewhere in a classic car, take her to the stage. They disappear to eat the flesh of near-extinct birds, reappear on the fringe.

She is the center, the earpiece and mouthpiece combined. The men like friends like men play mobile instruments. She tells everyone who's in charge. They know. They remember getting lost in all the lakes, her throwing them a raft of melody. She treats them like friends, lets them joke with her about her body. She turns into a clock so they can keep time, swivels her hips to keep the planet from standing still. When she slides left, they slide left. This is the new equilibrium. When she pops and locks, they pop and lock. This is the new eclipse. When she bows, they applaud. This is the new moon, the new tide.

Valerie

The recessed attacked the act of defiance, throwing rocks at his name on the big-city marquee. All that was left was S E E WIN   D. Most of them had been kindled by the spell, the cult-speak rhetorical question that asked if they were free. He had sent sound waves beyond allowable frequencies, bleats of synthetic lambs that seduced, prehistoric memes. They bought positivity pressed into vinyl and plastic whenever they saw a chance.

Dancing alone, he had poked a hole in stock markets, shiny thin ties poured into a wormhole. When he returned from exile, not a line appeared in his face, greased love coiling around the ravages of nostalgia. Some would cross the de facto picket line, toss three figures to ticket takers, remark about the voice that hadn't swallowed a single IOU, the voice that stayed in it for the fans.

Affair of the Heart

Everyone besides you learns to look in the mirror for reflections of what they've never been. You see only the horror of a pretty face that won't change. You wake from a nightmare, take the four-measure pause to believe what you lived wasn't real. You peek through the blinds to pinch yourself but glimpse a tiger, a stereotype. To give back to the fans, you let women pose for pictures with your childhood. You smile as they run their fingers through what's left of REM sleep. You let go of the accent as if it were your first love. You can't talk in dreams because a guitar solo screams through your mouth, your wax figure O. You know mirrors hide what it means to be alone because people laugh at you on the other side, people who reflect. You see the most of yourself in what you lose.

Love My Way

It was to be a contract killing, half the cash up front, half after rock & roll had been painted over and viewed in an open casket. Their weaponry wrapped nuance in cliché, promoted the xylophone to lead instrument. Water and sky, that ubiquitous duet of blue, would tenderize the landscape into three-chord submission. Tides would shake them up, spoiling their teen-mag faces with toxic waves. As they reached the bridge, their expressions stretched into gum on a playground. They could no longer go through with it, took themselves apart like revolvers. With new hooks in place, their menace of abandoned garages restored, they walked away prepared to face hordes of amplified plastic, all the malignant trends.

Love Is a Battlefield

You might not know what's linear. Of course it's time to run, time to grow up because you're ready. You'll think on a bus, think about making it in the arts. Even a non-dancer like you can learn enough moves to satisfy men who can't love. Some men stand up during gunfire with nothing in their hands. The only thing you do that your parents want you to do is stay safe. When one of the other women gets pulled by the boss, the golden-toothed reptile, you rally. You lead them in a shake of shoulders, the arc of a grenade. After the shrapnel of drink has torn away the boss' face, it's time to run again, to lead the way down an unwatched street. As you grow up once more, you're back on the bus, if you ever left the bus at all.

Suburbia

You start each sentence with *before*, a nod to the nostalgia of people who act like they didn't win. You picture a city without crime, a city with more people who speak your language. In books, the hardest choice used to be what hat to wear, which vegetable paired best with which meat from a once-living being. You love the highway bypass high above the city, the route that avoids check cashers, tax preparers, furniture rentals. There's so much to skip between work and home. Twenty minutes from the city, the city, your neighborhood comforts you with dogs that roam the streets, dogs that feast on unfinished business. You retire to the safety of home, the living room surrounded by boxes you won't open. The downtown you boarded up, the communities you filed under *after*, they know everyone by name, know whose backs to watch.

Marlene on the Wall

Friends couldn't keep up with her. It's one thing to be supportive, another to watch her turn from man to woman to man to woman to doors that open when she falls backward. She loved music but never sang along, fearful the wrong voice would come out. Mirrors had to go. She obscured them with posters of movie stars, posters that looked the same from any angle. The gangster's moll blew smoke that never lifted. She came up with a plan to make someone just like her, tearing down the posters, gluing them to life-size cardboard. The stars would skip, man-woman-man-woman, pages of a flipbook covered with doors. Motion would smolder in tuxedos and gowns. When she was done, her heavy twin could barely stand up, leaned against the window like a stalker of stalkers.

Now people peered in again, stared at something that didn't scare them. They rang the doorbell. She stayed one way long enough to keep them from scurrying. Everybody understood, lifted the leaden object, let go in unison. They watched identities run into themselves as the welcoming doors kept them inside.

She Bop

They met where times collide, at the drive-in that serves altered meat. She had been going solo, about to serve time for too many visits to the danger zone. He had pretended not to brag about the rocket he straddled like a pro. They skipped past drones that wielded serving-tray scythes, late-payment penalties pending. Speech had served little purpose, reserved mostly for people who claimed they invented feeling and its destruction; he and she had to expel metal shavings beforehand. Once they got going, it was as if they had forgotten how close forever had become. She had just been turned into a children's cartoon, stretched like taffy, returned to three dimensions, but he couldn't tell. Courtship progressed as mandated, a gathering of repurposed drones in the chorus. The newly together sported white suits and hats, danced a little, waited for the right moment to escape tyranny under a rainbow of raised canes.

Tong Poo

The powers warned us about eggs breaking. They slipped us into tuxedos, trained us to carry computers with the safeties unlocked. *Shake the palettes until the colors die*, they said. *Blend until smooth.* When you've lived your life in Stockholm syndrome, you never blink away the afterimage of hearts. Beneath our white shirts lay metal teeth so they could zip and unzip our rib cages to back up their floppies. *We will protect you*, they said, erecting gates with no fences around them. When the lights flashed COMPOSE, we wrote furiously on keyboards and electronic drums, crafted cool beverages in blenders, a smuggled hint of chrysanthemum in each sip. They had slipped needles through our skulls to remove the clouds of bombs, but they struck the places where fear grows like wayward exponents. We continued to sneak like a chop shop: contraband arpeggios, Akebono scales hidden beneath silken hammers. When the loops consoled our shivering sounds, all the dozens crashed, giving birth to only perfect birds.

I Can't Wait

Since the smog stole their light, her dog has had no use for eyes. She had sneaked her tools in his chew toy, wrenches rolled on drivers. She told them the urns were Mom and Dad's ashes. They didn't check, didn't see the inner frameworks. In the last days of alliteration and rhyme, she had learned lefty loosey, righty tighty. There was no mnemonic for altering the shape of gravity. She would turn all the pendulums to metronomes, set them at 90 beats per minute. Time would become currency. Anyone who needed to flee could buy a small piece of allegro or presto to skip past the powers' permanent andante. She needed to tweak the portion size so days would not end early. Ultimately, she would like to turn magnetism into reins, slow down the turbines, clear the skies. She would return light to its proper speed, set the blinders on fire.

Hero Takes a Fall

At first none of it worked. *In a perfect world* remained hypothetical, small change tossed in a busker's case. Then the men started to disappear. Women stopped wrapping themselves in sheets. They embraced atonal fashion: pumps with socks, stripes competing against shapes that lied and said they were parallel. Women conversed and cuddled with man-size Kens in business suits and Hawaiian shirts, caressed hollow hands till they fell off. Real men used to nod while pretending to listen. When dummies nod, they tip over. Their heads shatter. Women stand on a corner, but not in the way men used to think. Now they plug in guitars, belt four-part harmonies, attract the nodders who get it. Large bills run out of the case onto the street, cash to replenish all the broken accessories.

Doctor! Doctor!

Falsetto harmonies fill the prison, the planetarium where the moon is always out. The one woman worries about dementia, says the doctors will give it to you to make their money. She can still find the right notes on tympani, marimbas. The keyboard player turns red from the steam, the steam they pump in to keep the band moving. How could anyone sleep at a time like this? When they're not rehearsing for the next No. 1, they play cards with four decks, lead singer partnered with a mannequin. Everyone talks about health, about people they used to see, cousins who came over to talk about who got sick. If they talk about food, it's what they can't have anymore, what's poison, what died in the extinct soil. The singer says dementia is always real but the drugs might not be. They begin to curl up, to lower their heads when the keyboard player leaps from his chair. The perfect 16-measure solo has made its way into his head, his shadow shouted from an artificial star.

Waiting for a Star to Fall

The oldest story: first boy meets first girl. Boy tries to figure out how he works. Girl tries to figure out how she works. Each tries to figure out how each other works. They learn which pick-me-up glances work best. One of them invents the piano so they can write songs together. They blow giant bubbles, not knowing what they are so not dreading the pop, the disappearance. When they run on the beach in slow motion, the water ceases to terrify. At first they mate, then make love, at first to create a saxophone player for the solo, then children for photos.

Years pass. His hairline has begun to recede, but he grows it long in back, asks her if she likes it. She says *of course* without making eye contact. This is why they came up with sunglasses. Now even the flowers have outgrown them. She crafts black dresses susceptible to salt water and ice cream. He gets the message, tries by himself to re-create what they had done together, to craft hits for ill-fated divas. Instead, he just looks up and wonders why they stay, why light continues to lie to him long after the stars have died.

What's on Your Mind (Pure Energy)

We created interference. With all the quick cuts, they couldn't tell who was who. My memories, those times I swam in the ocean that burned, they mixed with hers, hours locked in the room where all she could do was read, read. We wrapped cardboard messages around our cerebra, fashioned guitars and violins from pool noodles, no frequencies necessary. When we thought too hard, we pantomimed hammers to heads, forgot all the recipes for hits. I was the one tasked with bleaching graffiti to the roots, designing the perfect *move on, nothing to see here* haircut. We dabbled in the narcotics that made our kidneys guffaw, expelled nursery school wallpaper, crass colors to sprinkle on ice cream. We dared them to *Go ahead: Try to know what we're thinking.* I counted from four down to zero before thumbing cataracts in their electric eyes.

Don't Dream It's Over

In the intro, he shrugged at friends who called him a savior, knew they had confused the testaments. His band should've been done in by plagues: note cards, frying pans, chicken on a stick that rained for days. He calmly walked through the house of verses, exorcising with acoustic guitar and floating head. Tropospheric dinner plates would shatter, first on the roof, later against the brazen openings of windows. He suggested they do chores until the storm passed, wield irons to smooth out shirts and ghosts. When he got to the last room, the final measures of song, he whispered in the drummer's ear: *Hold all my calls*. Finally he could set down the guitar, open the door to a projectile-free outro, stride into a meadow that reached to the end of the decade.

Acknowledgments

Thanks to the editors of the following journals in which some of these poems originally appeared in slightly different versions:

Across the Margin

Bitterzoet Magazine

Chiron Review

concis

Down in the Dirt

Drunk in a Midnight Choir

Eunoia Review

EXPOUND

Forklift, Ohio

Hermeneutic Chaos Literary Journal

Jet Fuel Review

Leopardskin & Limes

Maudlin House

Menacing Hedge

Mixtape Methodology

The Mondegreen

Newfound

Pittsburgh Poetry Review

scissors & spackle

Sonic Boom Journal

Unbroken

Uppagus

About the Author

Daniel M. Shapiro is the author of several poetry books and chapbooks, including *How the Potato Chip Was Invented*, *Heavy Metal Fairy Tales*, and *The Orange Menace*. He is a special education teacher who lives in Pittsburgh.

About the Artist

Stephen Tornero is a textile artist and art educator. He teaches Fashion Design and Visual Art to 7th and 8th graders while pursuing his own weaving practice and showing work at galleries and museums. He currently lives and works in Ohio and has a M.A. in Art Education from Kent State University.

Also published by bd-studios.com

Poetry Books

Georgia Dusk by Dudgrick Bevins & luke kurtis

Route 4, Box 358 by Dudgrick Bevins

Train to Providence by William Doreski & Rodger Kingston

Angkor Wat by luke kurtis

exam(i)nation by luke kurtis

the immeasurable fold by luke kurtis

Artists' Books

The Animal Book by Michael Harren

Tentative Armor by Michael Harren

Here Nor There by Sam Rosenthal

Just One More by Jonathan David Smyth

Architecture and Mortality by Donald Tarantino

The Male Nude by Michael Tice

Retrospective by Michael Tice

www.ingramcontent.com/pod-product-compliance
Lightning Source LLC
Chambersburg PA
CBHW041129110526
44592CB00020B/2744